METANOIA FOR GUYANA

Post Parris Electoral Conjectures

HASLYN PARRIS

Order this book online at www.trafford.com
or email orders@trafford.com

Most Trafford titles are also available at major online book retailers.

Printed in the United States of America.

ISBN: 978-1-4907-1651-0 (sc)
ISBN: 978-1-4907-1650-3 (e)

Trafford rev. 10/08/2013

www.trafford.com

North America & international
toll-free: 1 888 232 4444 (USA & Canada)
fax: 812 355 4082

Contents

In previous publications I have been at pains to highlight the fact that there is the likelihood of difficulties associated with anyone behaving like a heretic, dissenting from traditional beliefs and theories, challenging as inappropriate the views and decisions of the powers that be, and daring to specify publicly changes that ought to be pursued by the society. In support of the view that there is the likelihood of these kinds of difficulties occurring, I have provided a variety of evidence (comprising philosophical utterances and actual occurrences) that the phenomenon occurs repeatedly.

For instance, I have quoted the views of several distinguished philosophers (e.g. Machiavelli); or of distinguished writers (e.g. Ivan Van Sertima, editor of **'Great Black Leaders: ancient and modern'** on the back cover of which he states the view ***". . . that disaster seems to stalk anyone who challenges things as they are in the hope of transforming them into things as they should be."***; or of Doctors Herant Katchadoutian and Donald Lunde who on Page 12 of their book **'Fundamentals of Human Sexuality'** offer the caution that those who refuse to conform or make some attempt to change others' behaviour ***"should remember that deviation from the norm and forging ahead of one's time are the prerogatives of prophets and fools. One must be sure of his calling."***

I have also referred to the difficulties that have actually beset persons who have ignored the strong resistance to change by the powers that be, have been treated as heretics, and have paid the price for supporting or fomenting dissent.

Thus I have cited the fate of **Hypatia**, the daughter of Theon. She was a mathematics professor at the University of Alexandria, who was famous as an outstanding mathematical problem-solver. There are two statements attributed to her that supported the notion that she was intransigently pagan. They are as follows:

> *"Reserve your right to think, for even to think wrongly is better than not to think at all."*

And

"To teach superstitions as truth is a most terrible thing."[1]

Cyril, the patriarch of Alexandria, who pursued a strategy of oppressing philosophers, scientists and mathematicians, all of whom he considered heretics, must have been incensed by these statements. In 415, according to the historian Edward Gibbon: ***'On a fatal day, in the holy season of Lent, Hypatia was torn from her chariot, stripped naked, dragged to the church, and inhumanely butchered by the hands of Peter the Reader and a troop of savage and merciless fanatics; her flesh was scraped from her bones with sharp oyster-shells, and her quivering limbs were delivered to the flames.'***

There was also the case of **Hippasus** of Metapontum who, having discovered that the square-root of 2 cannot be expressed as a rational number (i.e. the ratio of two integers), insisted that 'irrational' numbers exist. He thereby flew in the face of Pythagoras' intuitively satisfying characterization of the universe in terms of rational numbers, incurred Pythagoras' wrath, and paid the penalty of being sentenced to death by drowning.

Similarly, around 1615, Galileo Galilee's support for the Copernican theory of the solar system centered on the Sun, with Earth and other planets moving around it, led to problems with the Inquisition, and serious harm to him was avoided only because of his friendship with Maffeo Cardinal Barberini who was named Pope Urban VII.

Antoine-Laurent Lavoisier was not as lucky. In May 1794, five years after the start of the French Revolution, he lost his head on the guillotine despite his scientific stature[2] (*cf. his then new oxygen theory of combustion displacing by 1785 the erroneous acceptance of Georg Ernst Stahl's phlogiston theory, although he did not lose his head directly because of that*).

I also here refer to the mathematician ***Adrien-Marie Legendre*** (then in his early seventies), who because he failed to support the government candidate for the Institut Nationale, had his pension stopped and eventually

1 Hypatia would have vehemently objected to the teaching embodied in the Catechism of the Catholic Church.

2 Joseph-Louis Lagrange was moved to comment: ***"It took them only an instant to cut off that head, and a hundred years may not produce another like it."***

became destitute. In 1824 Legendre refused to endorse the government's candidate for the *Institut Nationale des Sciences et des Arts* (the reopened French Academy of Sciences) and lost his pension from the *École Militaire*, where he had served from 1799 to 1815 as the mathematics examiner for graduating artillery students.

On 7 November 1837, Elijah Parish Lovejoy, American newspaper editor of the St. Louis Observer, was murdered. He had used his editorial position to strongly condemn slavery and to support gradual emancipation, in defiance of advice by important men in St. Louis, Missouri, who had written him a letter that requested him to moderate the tone of his editorials. Missouri was then a slave state. On the night of November 7, 1837, a mob attacked the building to which he had been forced to move his printing press across the Mississippi river into Alton, Illinois (Illinois was a free state) and he was killed while defending the building against that attack. His death in these circumstances strengthened the abolitionist movement.

On 26 May, 1521, the German priest and scholar, Martin Luther, was declared an outlaw and a heretic by the Edict of Worms which rejected Luther's proposed church reforms. These were Gospel-centered reforms within the Western Catholic church; and Luther's writings were forbidden. Luther had been excommunicated by Pope Leo X who had issued the Papal bull, *Decet Romanum Pontificem*, on 3 January 1521.

In 1925, the legislature of Dayton Tennessee, U.S.A., declared unlawful the proselytizing of any doctrine denying the divine creation of man as taught by the Bible. The conviction and fining of the high-school teacher, John T. Scopes[3], for teaching Charles Darwin's theory of evolution was justified by this law. The law was formally repealed only as late as 1967; although custom and practice allowed a blind eye to be applied to its existence.

Perhaps the most recent pertinent example of these types of difficulties is that of Nelson Mandela. His efforts to end apartheid in South Africa led to his imprisonment from 1962 to 1990. It is true that his persistence led not only to these difficulties but also to his being awarded the Nobel Peace Prize jointly with F.W. de Klerk in 1993; but the difficulties did occur.

---

3 The case was tried during July 10 to 21 of 1925 and was popularly known as the "Monkey Trial". On appeal Scopes was acquitted on the technicality of his US$100 fine having been excessive.

The effect of this litany of traumatized dissenters should, however, be relieved somewhat by noting the possibly blasphemous description accorded by the Swedish physician and psychiatrist, Axel Munthe, to Jesus Christ. He described Christ as *'an anarchist who succeeded'*. I am however unsure about how much of that success should be attributed to the dimension of parentage as evidenced by the statement *"This is **My** beloved Son, in whom I am well pleased."* [Matthew Chapter 3, Verse 17—After the Baptism of Jesus by John the Baptist]; and there **was** the subsequent occasion of the recorded plea *"Eloi, Eloi, lama sabachthani?"* [Matthew Chapter 27, Verse 46]

I have made a few decisions as a result of being faced with the caution stated as follows by Machiavelli in 'The Prince" in 1513:

> ***"It must be remembered that there is nothing more difficult to plan, more doubtful of success, nor more dangerous to manage than the creation of a new system. For the initiator has the enmity of all who would profit by the preservation of the old institutions and merely lukewarm defenders in those who would gain by the new ones. The hesitation of the latter arises in part from the fear of their adversaries, who have the laws on their side, and in part from the general skepticism of mankind which does not really believe in an innovation until experience proves its value. So it happens that whenever his enemies have occasion to attack the innovator they do so with the passion of partisans while the others defend him sluggishly so that the innovator and his party are alike vulnerable.***
>
> ***On this subject it is further necessary to inquire whether such innovators can rely on their own strength or must depend on others, that is, whether they must ask for help of others to carry on their work or can use force. In the first case they always come to a bad end and accomplish nothing but when they can depend on their own strength and are able to use force they rarely fail."***

This caution and the real life examples stated above have supported my arriving at the following decisions:

(1) I should not consider myself to be either a prophet or a fool;
(2) I should recognize that there exists and persists an irresistible force for evolutionary change in the affairs of man;
(3) I should be prepared to accept that the evolutionary process mentioned in (2) implies that there does **not** exist any system of governance, good for all time and appropriate for all circumstances, that therefore should be argued for as how things should be[4];
(4) I should be prepared to accept as true the maxim of Duc de la Rochefoucauld which states: ***'We have not the strength to follow our reason all the way.'***[5]; and
(5) I should, despite (4), do everything I can to follow the dictates of reason in my own life.

With respect to the fifth decision cited above, I have made it despite the circumstance that it appears that we have been advised by at least one person inspired by God that we should on occasion ignore our reason. Here I refer to what has become known as the GOLDEN RULE *(cf. Matthew 7:12 in the Holy Bible—the New Revised Standard Version by the Catholic Truth Society).* There, the Golden Rule is stated as: "***In everything do to others as you would have them do to you; for this is the law and the prophets.***"

Acceptance of this 'golden rule' as a panacea flies in the face of reason in at least two ways. First, given the prevalence of uncertainty about what's best for one's self, there is no reliable guide as to how one might apply this rule in a large number of situations. The rule's status of being universally applicable is thus suspect, despite its holy origins. Second, given the vagaries of individual preferences that may fly in the face of a society's current laws, the rule may provide justification for unacceptable behaviour, so-called 'perversions'. For example, deviant preferences such as masochism could justify sadism; or voyeurism could justify exhibitionism; or for liking being buggered could justify buggering, and *vice versa*.

---

4 John Stuart Mill had recognised this and had commented that: *'a true system of political philosophy should supply, not a set of model institutions but principles from which the institutions suitable to any given circumstances might be deduced.'*

5 This refers to the not infrequent *'exaltation of feeling and instinct over reason'.*

Among the conclusions to which I have been led by the quintet of decisions cited above, is that the concept of **'ethnicity based on race'** constitutes an inadequate basis for analyzing and prescribing for models of governance in Guyana. That concept is adequate as a basis for interesting debates and disquisitions[6]; but it is **useless** for anything other than generating arguments, causing confusion, and inhibiting cooperation **by virtue of its inherent inadequacies, illogicalities and contradictions**. Further, the concept is pernicious, especially since it is part of the foundation for a mental model that conflicts with pursuit of the objectives of Guyana's constitution.

Our slave masters and colonizers understood that 'ethnicity' was particularly useful for divisive purposes. For instance, they knew that the slaves obtained from Africa belonged to different ethnic groups; and, as stated in his Article 'The Berbice Revolt, 1763-64', the Guyanese historian Alvin O. Thompson notes ***". . . . Ethnic antagonisms were not unknown in slave society and many planters tried to ensure an ethnic mix among their slaves precisely in hope that this would help to keep slave society weak and divided."*** [7] Thompson, in the same Article stated that ***"The Amerindians also played an important role against the Africans by acting as the military auxiliaries to the Whites."***

Indeed, the whole tactic of highlighting and exploiting the heterogeneity of ethnicity as a device of a wider strategy of 'divide and rule' was designed and entrenched by the Dutch, the British, and other colonizers. Such colonizers appear to have taken seriously the advice given by Willie Lynch in a speech to some slave owners in 1712 on the bank of the James River in the colony of Virginia about how to make a slave. The Appendix to this Introduction gives some further detail about this reference to Willie Lynch.

---

6 The Stabroek News often carries good examples of this. For instance, the edition of Tuesday, May 29, 2012 carries the article entitled *'Panday knocks Indo-Trinidadians: Where's your self-respect?'* on Page 3; and on Page 7 there is the letter entitled: *'Indian-Guyanese were always keen on education but many lacked the economic capacity to send their children for secondary education'*.

7 Page98,second paragraph, of the 2009 publication by Hansib Publications **'Themes in African-Guyanese History'**, edited by Winston F. McGowan; James G. Rose; and David A. Granger. Mark you, avoidance of ethnic homogeneity was not sufficient to guarantee avoidance of revolt, both in Guyana and elsewhere.

I deem the matter of ethnicity based on race, and of the stereotypes associated with these ethnic categorizations, as being so important that I have devoted the first chapter of this book to highlighting the need for us to **abandon** use of the concept, particularly in our considerations of devising and operating systems of governance. Indeed, I deem the following statement, allegedly made by the British High Commissioner, on 17 May, 2011 on the occasion of the International Day Against Homophobia and Transphobia[8], to be relevant to the matter of ethnicity based on race, although this was clearly not his intended focus. The statement to which I refer is:

> *"And those laws and attitudes, of course, were reflected in the way Britain administered its former colonies, so we clearly have some historical responsibility for the legislation that countries like Guyana inherited at independence."*

We should note that the use of the concept **'ethnicity based on race'** was not an invention of race-conscious Guyanese, and certainly was not derived first in 1953 from the slogan **'Apan Jhaat'** as a competitive election strategy. The concept was a 'dubious gift', an inheritance from our colonial past based on the predispositions, preferences, philosophical urgings, impudent impostures and practices of our colonial masters to entrench a 'divide and rule' regime of managing the society—the very antithesis of encouraging cooperation among the ordinary people of the colony.

It is also imperative that readers of this book be forewarned of the author's predisposition to be an iconoclast. I am convinced that an attack on cherished beliefs is a necessary condition for orderly pursuit of many of the objectives of governance stated in Guyana's Constitution—e.g. Article 13 of that Constitution[9]. Avoidance of the jeopardy of embracing absurdities in the practice of governance, in the sense of avoiding participating in the ***'theatre of the absurd'*** as highlighted for instance in Samuel Beckett's

8 Cf. Page 13 of the Stabroek News of Wednesday, May 18, 2011.

9 Article 13 states: *'The principal objective of the political system of the State is to establish an inclusionary democracy by providing increasing opportunities for the participation of citizens, and their organizations in the management and decision-making processes of the State, with particular emphasis on those areas of decision-making that directly affect their well-being."*

Waiting for Godot or in Eugene Ionesco's *The Bald Soprano*, requires the will to reassess many cherished beliefs and practices. There is the need to embrace 'metanoia' in the original Greek sense. This book does not shy away from what the author considers necessary reassessments.

Appendix on Willie Lynch Letter

Willie Lynch was a British owner of slaves in the West Indies. He had been invited to the Colony of Virginia in 1712 to teach his methods to owners of slaves in the colony of Virginia and delivered the speech from which I quote on the bank of the James River in that colony. Lynch claimed that he had a fool-proof method for 'controlling your black slaves'; and that if that method were properly applied, 'it will control the slaves for at least 300 hundred years.' It may be interesting to note that **1712 + 300 = 2012, a**nd that Guyanese at all levels of intellectual achievement currently unabashedly use concepts of ethnicity and race to describe and analyze the society's condition!

He continued as follows: "My method is simple. Any member of your family or your overseer can use it. I have outlined a number of differences among the slaves; and I take these differences and make them bigger. I use fear, distrust and envy for control purposes. These methods have worked on my modest plantation in the West Indies and it will work throughout the South. Take this simple list of differences and think about them. On top of my list is "Age" but it's there only because it starts with an "A". The second is "Colour" or shade, there is Intelligence, Size, Sex, Sizes of plantations, Status on plantations, Attitude of owners, whether the slaves live in the valley, on a hill, East, West, North, South, have fine hair, coarse hair, or is tall or short. Now that you have a list of differences, I shall give you an outline of action. But before that, I shall assure you that *Distrust is stronger than trust and envy stronger than adulation, respect, or admiration.* The Black slaves, after receiving this indoctrination shall carry on and will become self refueling and self generating for HUNDREDS of years, maybe THOUSANDS. Don't forget, you must pitch the OLD black Male vs. the YOUNG black Male, and the YOUNG black Male against the OLD black Male. You must use the DARK skin slaves vs. the LIGHT skin slaves, and the LIGHT skin slaves vs. the DARK skin slaves. You must use the FEMALE vs. the MALE and the MALE vs. the FEMALE. You must also have your white servants and over-seers distrust all Blacks. But it is NECESSARY THAT YOUR SLAVES TRUST AND DEPEND ON US. THEY MUST LOVE, RESPECT AND TRUST ONLY US. Gentlemen, these kits are your keys to control. Use them. Have your wives and children use them. Never miss an opportunity. IF USED INTENSELY FOR ONE YEAR, THE SLAVES THEMSELVES WILL REMAIN PERPETUALLY DISTRUSTFUL. Thank you gentlemen."

> *[The term 'lynching' is derived from Willie Lynch's last name.]*

A not dissimilar set of ideas has been given by Carter Godwin Woodman in the publication *'The Mis-Education of the Negro'* as follows:

> *"If you can control a man's thinking you do not have to worry about his action. When you determine what a man shall think you do not have to concern yourself about what he will do. If you make a man feel that he is inferior, you do not have to compel him to accept an inferior status, for he will seek it himself. If you make a man think he is justly an outcast, you do not have to order him to the back door. He will go without being told; and if there is no back door, his very nature will demand one."*

CHAPTER 1

A Fundamental Rethink

The progress of societies/civilizations has been associated with the processes of the formulation, critique, and subsequent revision of various concepts. These processes may be considered as the evolution of thought, especially in the light of experience and as stimulated by political expediency; and are to be expected in each society / civilization. The processes have led, from time to time, to fundamental shifts in the way each society / civilization has defined and approached problems, to types of solutions that almost certainly would not otherwise have been formulated, and to the erection of platforms of understanding without which solutions to problems in the societies may even not have been proposed. Stasis in any dimension of thought can often inhibit the emergence of solutions to existing problems, foster the deepening of unwanted effects of those unresolved problems, and stimulate the emergence and growth of new problems not unrelated to the existence of the concepts that are in need of revision.

Admittedly, these paradigm shifts have not led to only blessings. They have also led to new problems—unintended and often unexpected side effects; but, even in the case of religious doctrines, the emergence of these effects has not justified acceptance of the idea that the process of revisiting current concepts should be avoided or abandoned.

Perhaps a few references to actual concepts and their revisions will help promote understanding of the process. The first reference I wish to make is to 'Phlogiston'.

Chemistry as we know that science today would almost certainly not have been, were it not for Antoine-Laurent Lavoisier's and others' revision of George Ernst Stahl's then well-regarded hypothesis (proposed around the beginning of the 18th century) that a common "fiery substance" he named "phlogiston" was released during combustion, respiration, and calcination, and that it was absorbed when these processes were reversed. Lavoisier found logical flaws in the popular hypothesis of the phlogiston theory. He did work between 1770 and 1790 that discredited the phlogiston theory. It was replaced by the oxygen theory of combustion even though chemists like the highly respected Joseph Priestly, who discovered oxygen in August 1774, stubbornly adhered to the phlogiston theory. By 1880 practically every chemist recognized the correctness of Lavoisier's oxygen theory, and had abandoned the phlogiston conjecture as logically flawed and unsupportable by experimental evidence in the laboratory.

A second example of a major paradigm shift relates to the matter of rational numbers. Pythagoras firmly believed and taught the principle that the universe was based entirely on 'rational numbers'. These are all numbers that could be expressed as the ratio of two whole numbers. The Pythagorean Brotherhood was shocked and incensed when the student Hippasus of Metapontum (around 450 BC) showed that the square root of 2 could not be expressed as any ratio of whole numbers. Instead of Hippasus' insight leading only to discussion, contemplation, and revision of the then accepted conjecture, it also led to Pythagoras venting his anger at the falsification of his fundamental beliefs. The inability of anyone, including himself, to find a flaw in Hippasus' proof about the square root of 2 further frustrated Pythagoras. It is alleged that he sentenced Hippasus to death by drowning. Eventually, Pythagoras' followers accepted the correctness of Hippasus' findings. What mathematics would have been like were the concepts of 'irrational numbers' and 'incommensurables' not to have been accepted is something I cannot imagine.

A not dissimilar matter concerns so-called imaginary numbers: numbers involving the square root of '-1', now often conventionally represented as '*i*'. Allegedly, these numbers were 'discovered' by European mathematicians in the 16th century. The paradigm shift that accepted the existence of imaginary numbers has facilitated a whole range of analyses from which today's modern 'civilized' societies have benefited—e.g. in matters related to alternating electric current.

In this matter of examples of paradigm shifts, I offer finally an experience in the field of medicine. It was Paracelsus (1493-1541) who spearheaded the rejection of the theory that good health results from the proper balance of four 'cardinal humours' (blood, phlegm, choler, and melancholy), and that disease results from an excess or an insufficiency of one or another of them. Paracelsus insisted that disease resulted from a specific cause outside the body. This alternative paradigm of Paracelsus underpins many of today's concepts of modern medicine[10]. Interestingly, a reassessment is currently taking place among psychiatrists, psychologists, and psychoanalysts, about how some situations have a psychic but not a material reality. The results may well point the way towards treating problems of phantom paralysis and pain.

Protagoras of Abdera, in Greece, was among the persons described by Plato and Aristotle as 'Sophists'. A person like Protagoras was thought of in the sense of being a *'captious or fallacious reasoner or quibbler'*. The presumption was that sophists are interested in winning arguments or debates as opposed to unearthing the 'Truth'. Unfortunately, man's willingness to indulge in paradigm shifts has often been thwarted by the attraction of the intellectual comfort of staying with what is currently believed, maybe based on a distrust of sophistry. Perhaps this is one of the reasons why many flawed concepts have had lives nearly centuries long. My hope is that the concept of **'ethnicity based on race'** as applied to Guyana in analyses of its current and projected economic and political affairs can be removed from that category of long-livers, and be accepted as otiose and pernicious.

The remainder of this chapter is dedicated mainly to highlighting that otioseness.

Perhaps the most fundamental flaw related to the concept of 'ethnicity based on race' (which is the concept used by Guyana's officialdom in the Bureau of Statistics) is the definitional reliance on ethnicity being expressible as discrete racial categories. Thus, even though provision has been made for a category named 'mixed', no scientifically applicable process has been specified for the determination of 'pure' ethnicities[11]. This logical gap needs to be closed in the context of more than a century

---

10 There still exist persons who attribute the causes of ailments such as 'White Mouth' and vaginal thrush not to vitamin deficiencies or to Candida albicans but to some obeah-like cause such as 'mashing' something and catching the 'jun juh'—which is **not** what Paracelsus had in mind.

11 Hitler's failures, experiences, and excesses in dealing with this concept of 'pure' races seem to have been lost on us. John Toland, Hitler's biographer, noted that Hitler, referring to America's concentration camps for Native American Indians, praised the efficiency of America's extermination—by starvation and uneven combat, as the model for his extermination of Jews and Gypsies.

of the opportunity for and the practice of miscegenation in the history of Guyana's population. The fact that one is dealing with fuzzy as opposed to crisp sets, involving degrees of belongingness to the ethnic categories specified, appears to have been ignored. Thus the genetic reality of a very large proportion of the population (almost certainly the overwhelming majority) qualifying for inclusion in the category 'mixed' has also been ignored.

Equally ignored are the vagaries of genetics that generate siblings whose physical appearances, including skin colour and hair texture, may be quite different from each other, even though the parental mix is deemed constant. They allegedly have the same mother and father; but may end up classifying themselves, or being perceived as belonging to different ethnic categories because they have different enough physical appearances. Indeed, if one focuses on cases in which the mother is the same, but there are different fathers[12], what I have called 'the vagaries of genetics' often produces a remarkable variability of skin colours and hair textures among half-brothers and half-sisters; with the variability itself varying over time as children grow up.

These kinds of problems are not unique to Guyana, and indeed pervade the thinking of many prestigious international institutions. Thus the UN declared the year 2011 (cf. the statement by Secretary General Mr. Ban Ki Moon) as the International Year for People of African Descent. There is a serious sense in which this statement flies in the face of the 'fact' that viewed zoologically, humans, Homo sapiens, are a culture-bearing, upright-walking species that lives on the ground and first evolved in Africa between 100,000 and 200,000 years ago. In the light of that alleged fact, a not unreasonable answer to the query: ***'Who are the people of African Descent?'*** might well be: ***'The whole world'***[13]. However, little has been

12 It has been estimated that paternity is unknown or incorrect in 3 to 10 percent of births in the United States. What the best estimate for Guyana might turn out to be is a quite fascinating question! Has 'blow' been more prevalent in Guyana than in the USA?

13 In 2000, Sterkfontein, located in Gauteng province, northwest of Johannesburg, South Africa, was declared a World Heritage Site on the basis of early hominid remains having been found there over the last few decades; and the area has been named 'the Cradle of Humankind'. However by 9 January, 2001 Australian scientists, on the basis of DNA from 60,000 year-old local human remains showing no links with human ancestors from

made of this incipient conundrum, and activities on an international scale have followed the declaration by Secretary General Mr. Ban Ki Moon, who I guess probably has the view that he is not of African Descent in the sense of his declaration.

Logically, we have gone this way before, as we did when we posed the question: 'Who is a Jew?' The fact is that a definition of 'Jew' satisfactory to all is almost impossible to construct, since it involves ethnic and religious issues that are both complex and controversial. Nevertheless we have persisted in using the term 'Jews' as though it is clear to whom it refers, and pay the consequent price of persistent confusion[14]. We do the same with so-called 'pure' ethnicities, e.g. white—an approach that allows as prestigious a publication as the 2007 edition of Encyclopaedia Britannica to state that ***"Janet Rosenburg Jagan was elected president of Guyana, becoming the first elected female president in South America and the first white president of Guyana"***.

Now we are using the term ***'People of African Descent'***. We are therefore poised to incur the penalties for accepting the imprecision leading: to illogicalities and contradictions; to intuition replacing reason in consonance with the Transcendentalism of Henry David Thoreau; and to accepting a basis for establishing stereotypes.

Given Guyana's current consensual and official acceptance of the type of ethnic/racial categories that our colonizers chose as the relevant categories to describe Guyana demographically, there are at least three sets of problems that arise.

The first relates to the adequacy of the categories defined. Can we avoid the implication that those categories which exist but that have not been identified as separate categories indeed comprise groups of lesser importance than those that have been identified? Thus, for instance, linguistically 'san-tan-tone' refers to persons of the mixture of African and Portuguese parentage. What justification does there exist for treating that category as less important than the separate categories 'African' and 'Portuguese' and therefore excluding it from the listing of specific

---

Africa, surmised that Africa might not be the only site of the genesis of the human species.

14 It was only as late as 8 December, 1998 that the United Nations General Assembly declared anti-Semitism a form of racism.

categories? A perhaps even more complex, and perhaps more unforgiveable omission, is the category 'boviander'[15] (a result of an Amerindian mother and a non-Amerindian, usually black or European, father)[16].

Second, the fuzziness of the categories leads to the question of cut-off points for membership of each category. There is the temptation, and possibly the practice, of considering that if a person appears to have more than x% 'African' in them *(x% is therefore defined as a minimum percentage)*they should be categorized as 'African' or 'Black'. However, this rule cannot be deemed acceptable for a given, fixed level of x% when it is also applied to 'East Indian', or 'Portuguese', or 'White', or 'Chinese'. The level of x% that qualifies a person to be categorized as 'black' may not suffice for also categorizing a person as 'white', since a person could then be simultaneously 'black' and 'white' without being 'mixed'! This kind of variability of the level of x% across categories has been fertile ground for many sorts of racial slurs and questionable categorizations. Many Guyanese (Georgetown based?) readers may recall the character 'Walker the Nigger' whose unwavering verbal response to being called that was: *"White, you damn fool, White"*, followed by the tossing of a well aimed brick at the person who had voiced that appellation.

I would be remiss if I did not mention that one implication of the illogicality of the definition is that 'African/Black' is treated as a case of contamination of otherwise 'pure' ethnicities. Also, the variability in the results of genetic mixtures supports the confusion inherent in terms like 'hard hair' and 'good hair'. All this highlights definitional inconsistencies and illogicalities inherent in the concept 'ethnicity based on race' and its application. These definitional inconsistencies and illogicalities should highlight and guarantee awareness of the technical inappropriateness for statistical purposes of categorization of people by using the concept ***'ethnicity based on race'***.

The third set of problems derives from the fact that the ill-defined and internally inconsistent concept of 'ethnicity based on race' stimulates and fosters thinking in stereotypical leaps based on our familiarity with life's

15 cf. Dictionary of Caribbean English Usage by Richard Allsopp.

16 The extra dimensions of complexity derive from the reality of the existence of several tribes ***(Arawak, Warau, Carib, Akawaio, Patamona, Arekuna, Makushi, Wapishana, and Wai Wai)*** of so-called Amerindians that have ethnic differences, e.g. they do not have the same language.

crisp sets. Thus we are familiar with crisp sets such as: **Birds** (Kiskadees, Blue Sakis, Gauldings, Chicken-hawks); **Fish** (Patwa, Houri, Banga Mary, Trout); **Fruits** (Sapodillas, Oranges, Guavas, Mangoes); **Insects** (Bedbugs, Acoushi Ants, Houseflies, Mosquitoes). There is almost[17] no miscegenation within or across these groups; and we **are** on good ground when we claim that we may not be able to 'define' a member of any of the sets, but we can recognize one when we see it. Thus we do not confuse Kiskadees with Blue Sakis or Gauldings or Chicken Hawks; and can say ***'Is so kiskadee stay',*** or ***'Is so Blue Saki stay'***, or ***'Is so Gaulding stay'***, or ***'Is so Chicken Hawk stay'***, and attach stereotypical characteristics to the members of each set of that type. Similar remarks are made about Fish, Fruits, and Insects, specifically expressing our individual perceptions, preferences, and disgusts. This kind of problem is not peculiar to Guyana, or indeed to the matter of race. Thus, for instance, in dealing with the 1964 case Jacobellis v. Ohio in the matter of **'obscenity'** the U.S. Associate Supreme Court Justice Potter Stewart uttered the following words in his concurring opinion in the case: *"I shall not today attempt further to define the kinds of material I understand to be embraced within that shorthand description; and perhaps I could never succeed in intelligibly doing so. But I know it when I see it."* For many of us, the last sentence of the quotation applies to the shorthand descriptions: **'coolie man'; 'black man'; 'buck man'; 'chinee man'.**

One immediate result of treating a fuzzy set like a crisp set is that analyses like those derived from the concept ***'ethnicity based on race'*** are a hopeless waste of intellectual effort **except in one important circumstance**. That circumstance is the one which occurs when a large number of persons think in terms of ethnicity based on race, and determine their competitive actions on the basis of their accompanying stereotypical beliefs:

> ***'Is so coolie people stay'; 'Is so chinee people stay'; Is so black people stay'; 'Is so buck people stay'; 'Is so buck and people stay'; 'Is so white people stay'; 'Is so putagee people stay'***.

17 The circumstance of various breeds of dogs signals the need for the caution of 'almost'; and I have a friend who swears that she has a fowl-cock that routinely treads her guinea-bird, with what results re guinea-bird eggs that might be hatched, she remains unsure.

These types of statements, which pervade our loose use of ordinary Guyanese language, and our perceptions of people in many dimensions of their expected and actual behaviour, comprise the basis of many interpersonal difficulties and delights[18].

The three sets of problems cited above have had historically various attempts made at their resolution. Thus, for instance, C.L.R. James in his book, **'The Black Jacobins'**, observes that in San Domingo, the attempt to categorize the offspring of white and black and intermediate shades led to the definition of 128 divisions. In that system of categorization, the ***sang-mêlée*** with 127 white parts and 1 black part was still a man of colour, demonstrating the inability to avoid the aspect of 'black' being a contaminant as mentioned above. Adolf Hitler's **Mein Kampf** dealt with similar categorization problems.

It is useful to highlight what we actually do, and have been doing for the longest while in Guyana. Certainly since the 1960 census (more than 50 years ago), and probably at least since 1946, we have collected statistics on ethnicity by race. There is also the practice that in between censuses, we collect that information as part of various National Surveys and other official statistics.

The definitional problems cited above are circumvented by the simple strategy of asking the respondent to say to what ethnic group by race the respondent belongs; and enumerators are not allowed to overrule respondents' self-classification[19]. Respondents are required to pick from a prepared list of categories. The only time when this strategy cannot but fail is when a deceased person's ethnicity has to be recorded. In the case of the 2002 Population and Housing Census—Individual Questionnaire, labeled B—the ethnic group categorizations supplied (cf. section P1.4) are: 1. **African/Black**; 2. **Amerindian**; 3. **East Indian**; 4. **Chinese**; 5. **Mixed**; 6. **Portuguese**; 7. **White**; 8. **Other(specify)**; 9. **Don't know/Not stated**. My understanding is that respondents are required to state into which one of these 9 categories they place themselves. It would be interesting to know into which category the most recently declared (2011) President of Guyana has placed himself, given the information supplied by his wife (cf. Pages 9 & 13 of Sunday Stabroek, Dec 11, 2011) that *'his mother was a mixture*

18 Allegedly hot-blooded 'dougla' or 'boviander' women are often compared with females of allegedly cooler-blooded 'pure' races.

19 This rule would certainly have earned the approval of 'Walker the Nigger'.

of African and Amerindian, and his father was Indian'; and into which category voters placed him as they considered the Presidential Candidates in the 2011 General Elections[20].

I have chosen to not investigate seriously whether the officially used categories have been invariant over time. That choice has been made because no such variation can avoid any of the following five dimensions of inappropriateness of the principle/concept 'Ethnicity based on Race' as a basis for serious analyses. These dimensions can be stated as follows:

1. The contradictions inherent in the definition of categories as one deals with Fuzzy as opposed to Crisp sets;
2. The stimulus that the attempted system gives to thinking in terms of stereotypes;
3. The stimulus that the categorization provides for the questions: *which category is/should be at the bottom of the ladder of material well-being*? and *which category 'deh pun top'*?
4. The fact that in Guyana's case, the system derives from a system devised by its colonizers to underpin the strategy of 'divide and rule'; and
5. The fact that the preceding four dimensions eschew cooperation as a strategy for pursuing national 'development'.

The rule that ought to be accepted and applied is that:

> *A sufficient condition for a principle/theory/conjecture* **not to be used** *for serious analyses underpinning policy making and action is that in it there inheres any logical inconsistency or contradiction.*

With respect to dimension (5) stated above, it is useful to note a principle well-understood by serious musicians. It is that:

> **'The sound and fury characteristic of a cacophony generated by the undisciplined competition of individual players warming up or seeking to outdo**

20 In this matter readers may find it interesting to note, and perhaps try to apply to the Guyana situation, the analogue of the principle that all Jews agree that a child born of a Jewish mother is Jewish; and that Reform Judaism affirms that a child is Jewish if either one of its parents is a Jew.

each other in pursuit of narrow individual objectives as opposed to collaborative group orchestral goals is to be studiously controlled.'

If the foregoing comments are accepted, then one unavoidable conclusion is that the use of the description of Guyana's population by ethnicity based on race **should be abandoned**[21]. This abandonment is a necessary, but not sufficient condition, for the successful pursuit of a collaborative, consensual effort aimed at Guyana's development. Not only should the Bureau of Statistics abandon the practice of data collection based on ethnic/racial categories, but also the authorities (including teachers and politicians) responsible for education should discontinue publishing books and teaching persons, particularly children, the concepts of to what ethnic group they belong. Certainly, children are not born with notions of to what ethnic group they belong—**they are taught it! Indeed, they are taught, formally and informally: the category to which they belong; the categories to which other people belong; and the stereotypes that are associated with the various categories, including their own.**[22] This is just **one** of the dimensions of mis-education enshrined in Guyana's formal education system. Unfortunately, the abandonment mentioned above[23], if adopted, will be manifested as exclusion from the mental models used by Guyanese only several (very many?) generations after the formal abandonment by officialdom![24]

---

21 The characterization of Guyana as a land of six peoples would then also have to be abandoned!

22 Thereby attempting to ensure that students become clones of Justice Potter Stewart mentioned above in the case of 'obscenity' in the sense of being able to say "But I know it when I see it". More importantly, Bohm has commented: *'Thus, a paradox which has taken root early in life (e.g. that arising out of a situation in which a child is made to feel a sense of inadequacy) may continue for the whole of a person's life, always changing in detail, growing more and more confused, but remaining the same in essence'.*

23 The type of abandonment being recommended is not novel! It has been done in relation to the categorization '***mestizo***' by Mexico which found the description so variable in meaning that it has been abandoned in census reports.

24 It is interesting to note that during 12th century anti-Semitism the uncertainties associated with defining who is a Jew led to the compulsory use of a yellow badge that identified the wearer as a Jew, a practice that was revived by the Nazis; and that the practice of segregating the Jewish populations of towns and cities into ghettos dates from the Middle Ages and lasted until the 19th and early 20th centuries in much of Europe.

In this respect, it is instructive to consider some comments made by Alan Lenzi (professor of religious studies at University of the Pacific who studies biblical numerology). He is reported to have noted that cognitive scientists have demonstrated that the human brain is hard-wired to look for meaningful patterns in the sensory data it collects from the world. He has explained that in most situations, this cognitive wiring helps us. It enables us, he notes, to pick important information out of a background of random noise; but sometimes we overdo it by finding patterns where they aren't—from faces seen in the clouds to numerical coincidence. Once found, the patterns are easily and often imbued with imaginative meaning[25], Alan Lenzi has claimed.

Nate Silver, in the Introduction of his book 'The Signal and the Noise', quotes Tomasso Poggio, an MIT neuroscientist who studies how our brains process information, as making similar relevant comments. Poggio allegedly has noted that *'This need of finding patterns, humans have this more than other animals'*; and that *'Recognizing objects in difficult situations means generalizing. A newborn baby can recognize the basic pattern of a face. It has been learned by evolution, not by the individual.'* Poggio allegedly goes on to say that the problem is that these evolutionary instincts sometimes lead us to see patterns when there are none there. *'People have been doing that all the time'*, Poggio allegedly said—*'Finding patterns in random noise.'*

It is this kind of predisposition that gives rise to stereotyping, once racial categories have been listed. Alleged similarities within categories are sought, perceived, and taught as true; as are differences between categories. These patterns of similarities and differences underpin the statements of the type *"Is so 'x' people stay"*[26]; and there is consensus born of formal and informal mis-education that treats the statements as revealed truths rather than as at best merely interesting conjectures.

25 Horoscopes seek to highlight these patterns, and it would be interesting to hazard a guess as to what meaning one should give to the numerical coincidence that Queen Elizabeth II of England and the Marquis de Sade have the same birthday—2 June—1926 and 1740 respectively. There is a similar coincidence involving Anne Bronte, sister of Charlotte and Emily, who was born on 17 January 1820, and the American gangster Al Capone who was born on 17 January 1899.

26 cf. Pages 46-54 of the book ***Parris Electoral Conjectures and Governance in Guyana*** by Haslyn Parris.

In this matter I am reminded of a story told by a wag. The story is based on the following arithmetical fact:

> Consider the ten integers 0, 1, 2, 3, 4, 5, 6, 7, 8, 9.
> Choose any three of them to form a three-digit number e.g. 486
> Reverse the digits to form a new three-digit number viz. 684
> Subtract the smaller number from the larger one—(giving 198)
> Reverse the digits of the number resulting from the subtraction—(giving 891)
> Add the last two results—thereby getting 1089

The arithmetical fact is that this sequence of operations will always produce the number 1089, for **any** three digits chosen.

Armed with this pattern, the wag exercised his active imagination and generated the following story about 39 nuns and one mother superior who all lived in the same convent, and each of whom could not sleep at night.

The mother superior asked a psychiatrist for help and he suggested the following approach to finding a solution:

Let's write down your problem, the psychiatrist said, as pithily as we can.

He then proceeded to write: S L E E P N I G H T

and then linked the ten numerals 0 1 2 3 4 5 6 7 8 9 with this problem statement, using the rationale that these numerals are the basis for forming any number[27], and therefore can be manipulated to generate the solution to the problem.

He invited the mother superior to choose any three integers from the 10 numerals; and had her go through the process described above[28], thereby

---

27 The psychiatrist must have been a descendant of Pythagoras.

28 He justified the rigmarole of her reversing numbers and adding and subtracting them as deriving from the need to walk all around the problem, to see it from all vantage points, especially given that she herself was experiencing the problem.

generating the number 1089. He then noted that there was one fact that had not been used—that fact being that there were 40 persons who had difficulty sleeping at night. He suggested that this fact be used by multiplying the derived number, 1089, by 40. This last step of the process yielded the result **43560**, which he claimed was the answer to the problem; and he explained that all the mother superior had to do was to use the link with the problem statement to go back from numbers to words. Thus '4' represented 'P', '3' represented 'E', and so on.

The mother superior complied and then asked whether the process used would always produce this answer, regardless of which three integers she chose. The psychiatrist, with a twinkle in his eye ignored the fact that her question was about arithmetic, and assured her that he could guarantee that the solution would always work.

Something akin to this degree of ridiculousness is bound to happen when an inappropriate principle is pressed into service; and **'ethnicity based on race'** ***is*** one such inappropriate principle. Clearly, a deeper rethink is required; and the following Chapter 2 addresses **some** of this in relation to the National Assembly, the highest forum of governance in Guyana.

The formal and informal education system to which all Guyanese have been exposed, to a lesser or greater degree, needs to have as an antidote the injection of information such as is contained in the book **"If you want to learn Early African History START HERE"**. This book was first published in 2010 by Reklaw Education[29]. I recommend it as **one** of the injections of information necessary to correct, for instance, the idea that Africa and its descendants needed to be rescued from their uncivilized (libidinous, near naked, drum beating) state—a dubious benefit of slavery. The book contains informative chapters on: **The Songhai Empire; Great Benin; The Kanen-Borno Empire; and the Munhumutapa Empire.**

It may be useful to draw attention to some actual examples that are disturbingly destructive of efforts to forge national cooperation. Such examples could only have resulted directly from mental models that lead to a fundamental belief in, and the application of, the inappropriate concept 'ethnicity based on race', and its implications based on stereotypes. These examples are provided in the appendices to this chapter. One deals with

29 The book is also available in e-book format for kindle type devices.

the editorial published by the Guyana Chronicle of 2nd July, 2012 entitled **"Opposition rampages to sow disunity in the country"**. Another is a compilation of official posts and names of the alleged occupants of those posts, designed to demonstrate the then ruling party's alleged preference for a certain ethnic group defined using the concept 'ethnicity based on race'. The expected mental link between surnames and ethnicity is, in that listing, relied on to determine the ethnicity of the individual with that surname[30]. These examples should not lead one to think that this stereotyping problem is confined to Guyana and Guyanese. The third example in the appendices refers to Jews, and the reader ought to be able to see the similarities. The fourth example is here given to invite the reader to apply the principle of the correlation between surnames and ethnicity to the conjecture that '**Golf in Guyana has been taken over by East Indians**'; and to highlight the '***ridiculousness***?' of that conjecture. The author of this book is convinced that the Article quoted in this fourth example **was in no way motivated by interest or belief in the conjecture by the Stabroek News.**

All of this kind of misleading analysis occurs because we have treated Sparrow's calypso ***'Dan is the Man in the Van'*** as a less than serious commentary on the scandalously inappropriate educational system we have persisted in using. It is this system that encourages us to treat 'ethnicity based on race' as a useful concept blessed by officialdom; even though the concept runs counter to many of the principles and objectives we have enshrined in our Constitution. Hopefully, by the time readers have completed their reading of this Chapter 1 and its Appendices, they will be ready to accept that a central dimension of reform (the **metanoia** to which the title of this book refers) ought to involve an official attack on the existence and use of the concept 'ethnicity based on race'.

30 This correlation is often accepted as reliable even in the face of evidence such as that in the Eversham/Kiltern area the surname 'Jaundoo', or in the area of Cromarty/#35,#36 Village Corentyne the surname 'Busgith', or in various areas of the USA the surname 'Soodoo', is not an unambiguous indicator of the ethnic/racial group to which the possessor of the surname belongs or would claim to belong.

APPENDIX 1 TO CHAP 1

Opposition rampages to sow disunity in the country

Monday, 02 July 2012

When the opposition goes on a rampage during its intermittent forays to make the country ungovernable, innocent people get hurt—badly. People who sacrificed much and worked hard all their lives to build and sustain businesses lose everything in minutes.

The PNC's great hero and candidate, Ronald Waddell, was caught on camera flush with a bucket at a gas station not far from where Regent Street was burning.

Black youths are socialised by opposition leaders to think that Indians robbed them to get rich, so they automatically feel that they have to wrest by force, even murder, anything Indians have. Hatred of Indians is ingrained into their psyche. Many Indian persons, who grew up in the arms of black people in rural communities have today become fearful anytime a black youth gets too close to them.

So the PNC did not only make Indians their victims, but they also made their own supporters their victims, because the most innocent, clean-living black youths are just as suspect as the perpetrators as a result of the difficulty to tell the difference between a criminal and a decent person.

When PNC leaders encourage young black men to attack members of the Indian community for gain and they experience the sweetness of freeness, it is merely a matter of time before they turn their voracious ways toward PNC supporters, which has been happening for a while now.

Today the hatred is being vented toward GuySuCo workers, on the wrongful premise that GuySuCo workers comprise only persons of Indian descent.

But there are a great number of PNC and AFC supporters who work in GuySuco who are being negatively affected from the political fallout.

The opposition leaders who encourage their supporters in Linden to feel that other Guyanese, including poor single mothers and old people struggling for their sustenance and that of their families should pay taxes and higher electricity rates so that electricity consumed by Lindeners could continue to be subsidised should remember that it is also opposition members throughout the rest of the country who are helping to sustain Linden's free use of electricity consumption, so this issue should not be one of politics, but of equitable rights for all Guyanese.

If anyone is to follow the trends of Guyana's political past, they would discover that an escalating crime wave and lobbying to derail developmental funding always correlate with this country's election season, and post-elections.

And, true to tradition, the opposition cabal is ramping up its diatribe against the PPP/C Government, which they are determined to remove—not necessarily by fair means—even taking their anti-nationalist, practically treasonous propaganda to international fora. As always, murderous criminal activities are rising in direct proportion.

Former President Bharrat Jagdeo had said, "Opposition should criticise the government when they make mistakes, and we are not perfect. We do make mistakes sometimes and that (criticisms) is fair; but to have an assault on the Guyanese people through distortions is another matter. To openly lie and peddle falsehoods is not a right of anyone, and that is not fair.

"If you listen to them carefully, their plans for Guyana—and for all of our people, is about what the PPP should or should not do—and it is all criticisms and negativity. They have never, ever presented a positive plan for fixing the problems of Guyana and for creating a better life for our people . . . . They criticise us in Parliament that we are spending too much money on housing. When we allocated $4 billion to buy some land from GuySuco to produce some (additional) 10,000 house lots for Guyanese, they made a big issue of it in Parliament, criticising Irfaan Ali for this (initiative). They know only about criticisms, but not about positive things . . . .

"We still have a long way to go, but we are getting there . . . . more and more people are benefiting."

But the joint opposition has no intention to allow government's developmental thrust to continue because this does not suit their agenda.

Instead, they are trying desperately to halt and/or reverse gains made through various stratagems, of which ramping up the inflammatory rhetoric—and the imbroglio over the electricity discord, with Lindeners being targeted as the latest cannon fodder, like they once used Buxtonians and their issues.

That the government's developmental and people-empowerment initiatives have been re-generating confidence in the administration, to the extent where communities in the opposition enclaves are reaching out with trust and hope to the administration for improved living conditions and enhanced lifestyles, is inimical to their self-interested and self-centred agendas for self-aggrandizement and self-empowerment, and they are attempting to destabilise this budding unity in the Guyanese nation, and the people's trust in the administration by whatever way possible, even to blaming the government for things which they (the opposition) are culpable.

Yes, too much is at stake, and care needs to be taken by the people in the country that the opposition forces do not succeed in their evil intentions by sowing seeds of strife in the land once more, because it is the Guyanese people whom they are hurting.

Last Updated on Monday, 02 July 2012

APPENDIX 2 TO CHAPTER 1

The following pamphlet must have been produced by persons in opposition to the PPP/C. Its objective is to demonstrate that the PPP/C is a racist organization bent on what the pamphlet calls 'Indianisation' of Guyana. The pamphlet's effectiveness is based on a reader having a mental model that includes the following three assumptions:

(i) Each person in Guyana can be categorized as belonging to the Categories "East Indian" and "Non East Indian", and there are known stereotypes accurately associated with those categorizations;
(ii) The surname of any person, except when acquired by marriage, is frequently a reliable indicator of whether that person is "East Indian";
(iii) Any Guyanese can be uniquely categorized as to whether they are "African" or equivalently "Black".

Any person whose mental model accommodates those assumptions, and whose thinking and consequent actions are based on such a mental model, can be categorized as **racist**. Unfortunately, because of education, the categorization described in the previous sentence is almost certainly true of most Guyanese, past and present, including our leaders, past and present, all of whom have been mis-educated to accept the model.

The pamphlet is a ridiculous, contumelious, document that can have resulted only from a mind that has accepted that the majority of Guyanese have the mental model with the characteristics described above.

Here is a **verbatim reproduction** of the Pamphlet. **I find its content and intent abhorrent!** Its author is unstated and unknown to me. No attempt has been made by me to correct anything I consider erroneous or preposterous:

"DONALD RAMOTAR

(Out of evil, cometh evil)

When Cheddie Jagan died in 1997, Donald Ramotar became General Secretary of the PPP. During Janet Jagan's tenure as president, the PPP hatched a Master Plan titled “The Indianisation of Guyana”. This plan called for East Indians to dominate and control every sector of the Guyanese society. The supremacy of the East Indian over the Black man was to be established and maintained. This was in keeping with the tenets of Hinduism that the Black man is lower than the lowest caste of East Indian. It was Donald Ramotar’s responsibility to oversee the implementation of this plan.

There was to be no development in Black areas of Guyana and the Government would marginalize Africans from benefitting from State sponsored ventures. Any area of Black dominance was to be de-emphasized, resulting in Linden becoming a depressed community.

Donald Ramotar oversaw the empowerment of East Indians in both the public and private sectors, even in areas of sports and recreation. East Indian appointments dominated the Cabinet, and every state board was given an East Indian chairman. These included Guyana Power & Light, Guyana Water Inc., Guysuco, Guycil, National Drainage & Irrigation Board among others.

All State Commissions were also given East Indian Chairpersons. These included the Public Service Commission, Teaching Service Commission, Judicial Service Commission, Public Utilities Commission, Forestry Commission, Guyana Elections Commission, among others.

The Govt facilitated the Drugs trade for the benefit of East Indian businessmen. It was for this reason that Yesu Persaud was made to set up Demerara Bank, to launder Drugs money, after his classical failure with GA 2000.

A programme to have only East Indian people get loans to buy trucks and then be given contracts on road building projects was directed and controlled by Donald Ramotar from Freedom House. Not one Black Man was included in this programme of over 400 trucks. There was even an effort to have an All Indian Guyana Cricket Team.

East Indian owned businesses such as Demerara Distillers Ltd., Hand in Hand, GBTI and even New Building Society, were given instructions not to employ Black People. There were fast track promotions for Indian officers in the Guyana Police Force and the GDF. All this was done and continues to be done under the watchful eye of Donald Ramotar, General Secretary and now Presidential Candidate of the PPP.

Black People were dismissed from the State owned media, TV, Radio and the Chronicle, and Indians were put in charge from CEO to announcer, to driver.

The Master Racist of the PPP is Donald Ramotar. He made the Government stop deducting union dues from the Public Service Union, a majority black Union, while allowing Guysuco to continue to deduct dues for the PPP union, GAWU.

He was a member of the Omai Board and used his influence and was paid to declare Omai not guilty of the cyanide spill, betraying all the people of Guyana who live along the Essequibo River and at Bartica.

Donald Ramotar has been the power source behind the PPP leading the assault to marginalize Black People. The attacks on the M&CC Georgetown, M&TC New Amsterdam and the M&TC Linden—the three big towns—are part of this plan. Yet the three minor towns of Anna Regina, Corriverton and Rose Hall, where Indians are in the majority, get larger subventions per capita than the big three from Central Government.

Donald Ramotar is quoted as saying that Black people were brought here as slaves and they do not have business sense, and they do not have the brains to run a country. Guyana must never be run by Black people again. Quoting Cheddie Jagan, he said "Black people are at the bottom of the social ladder and it is our duty to ensure they remain there." It is because of this that Jagdeo had to try to convince people that Ramotar is not a racist. All Black Guyanese, however, know better. The evidence is there for all to see.

Only a fool would believe that Guyana can develop, by developing only one race.

R—repression

A—against

M—men

O—of

T—the

A—African

R—race

1	Auditor General	Deodat Sharma
2	Finance Secretary	Nirmala Rekha
3	Registrar Supreme Court	Nibi Shabena Ali
4	Director of Public Prosecution	Shalimar Ali Hack
5	Chairman, Georgetown Public Hospital Corporation	Michael Khan
6	Chief Medical Officer	Shamdeo Khan
7	Director Regional Health Services	R. N. Singh
8	Director General, Civil Aviation Authority	Zulficar Mohammed
9	Chairman, Guyana Elections Commission	Steve Surijbally
10	Chief Elections Officer	Gocool Budhoo
11	Chairman, Guyana Energy Agency	Doorga Persaud
12	CEO, Guyana Energy Agency	Mahander Sharma
13	Chairman, Guyana Forestry Commission	Tarachand Balgobin
14	Head, Customs Anti Narcotics Unit	Girvam Singh
15	Commissioner, Guyana Forestry	James Singh
16	CEO, Guyana Lands and Survey Commission	Doorga Persaud

17	Head, Value Added Tax & Excise Dept	Hema Khan
18	Chief Hydrometerological Officer	Bhaleka Seulall
19	Chairman, Public Service Commission	Ganga Persaud
20	Chairman, Police Service Commission	Dennis Morgan
21	Pro Chancellor, University of Guyana	Prem Misir
22	Chairman, Guyana Power & Light	Mike Brassington
23	CEO, Guyana Power & Light	Bharrat Dindial
24	Chairman, Guyana Sugar Corporation	Nanda Bopaul
25	Chief Labour Officer	Yoganand Persaud
26	CEO, Berbice River Bridge	Omadat Samaroo
27	Chairman, National Drainage and Irrigation Authority	Walter Willis
28	Chairman, Police Complaints Authority	Cecil Kennard
29	Chairman, Public Utilities Commission	Prem Persaud
30	Chairman, Teaching Service Commission	Leila Ramson
31	Programme Director, National Communication Network	Martin Goolsaran
32	CEO, National Communication Network	Mohammed Sattaur
33	Head, Government Information News Agency	Neaz Subhan
34	Head, National Frequency Management Unit	Valmikki Singh
35	Speaker of the National Assembly	Ralph Ramkarran
36	Permanent Secretary	Nigel Dharamlall

37	Director of Youth & Sports	Neil Kumar
38	CEO, Cheddie Jagan International Airport	Ramesh Gheir
39	Minister of Agriculture	Robert Persaud
40	Minister of Culture, Youth & Sports	Frank Anthony
41	Minister of Education	Sheik Baksh
42	Minister of Finance	Ashni Singh
43	Minister of Housing & Water	Irfaan Ali
44	Minister of Health	Leslie Ramsammy
45	Minister in the Ministry of Health	Bherri Ramsarran
46	Minister of Labour	Manzoor Nadir
47	Minister of Human Services	Priya Manickchand
48	Minister of Legal Affairs	Charles Ramson
49	Ambassador to Brazil	Kellowan Lall
50	Minister of Tourism, Industry & Commerce	Maniram Prashad
51	Chairman GGMC	Joe Singh
52	CEO Civil Defence Commission	Chabilall Ramsarup
53	PS Min of Education	Philander Khandal

THE INDIANISATION OF GUYANA: Master plan of the PPP.

House Slaves: Roger Luncheon, Samuel Hinds, Robeson Benn, Odinga Lumumba, Kwame Gilbert, Keith Burrowes, Kwame McKoy, Henry Greene, James Rose, Juan Edghill."

APPENDIX 3 TO CHAPTER 1

This is a totally scandalous and disgusting article posted on the internet. It is conceptually based on the presumption that there is clear definition of who is a 'Jew', and seeks to establish a stereotype of a highly intelligent group to which the whole world is/should be indebted. It should be interesting to note that the first volume of Hitler's Mein Kampf, entitled ***DieAbrechnung*** and written in 1924, identified the Aryan as the "genius" race and the Jew as the "parasite", the very opposite of what follows.

Iran's Supreme Leader Grand Ayatollah Ali Khomenei urged the Muslim World to boycott anything and everything that originated with the Jewish people.

In response, Meyer M. Treinkman, a pharmacist, out of the kindness of his heart, offered to assist them in their boycott as follows:

> "Any Muslim who has Syphilis must not be cured by Salvarsan discovered by a Jew, Dr. Ehrlich. He should not even try to find out whether he has Syphilis, because the Wasserman Test is the discovery of a Jew. If a Muslim suspects that he has Gonorrhea, he must not seek diagnosis, because he will be using the method of a Jew named Neissner.

"A Muslim who has heart disease must not use Digitalis, a discovery by a Jew, Ludwig Traube.

Should he suffer with a toothache, he must not use Novocaine, a discovery of the Jews, Widal and Weil.

If a Muslim has Diabetes, he must not use Insulin, the result of research by Minkowsky, a Jew. If one has a headache, he must shun Pyramidon and Antypyrin, due to the Jews, Spiro and Ellege.

Muslims with convulsions must put up with them because it was a Jew, Oscar Leibreich, who proposed the use of Chloral Hydrate.

Arabs must do likewise with their psychic ailments because Freud, father of psychoanalysis, was a Jew.

Should a Muslim child get Diphtheria, he must refrain from the "Schick" reaction which was invented by the Jew, Bella Schick.

"Muslims should be ready to die in great numbers and must not permit treatment of ear and brain damage, work of Jewish Nobel Prize winner, Robert Baram.

They should continue to die or remain crippled by Infantile Paralysis because the discoverer of the anti-polio vaccine is a Jew, Jonas Salk.

"Muslims must refuse to use Streptomycin and continue to die of Tuberculosis because a Jew, Zalman Waxman, invented the wonder drug against this killing disease.

Muslim doctors must discard all discoveries and improvements by dermatologist Judas Sehn Benedict, or the lung specialist, Frawnkel, and of many other world renowned Jewish scientists and medical experts.

"In short, good and loyal Muslims properly and fittingly should remain afflicted with Syphilis, Gonorrhea, Heart Disease, Headaches, Typhus, Diabetes, Mental Disorders, Polio Convulsions and Tuberculosis and be proud to obey the Islamic boycott."

Oh, and by the way, don't call for a doctor on your cell phone because the cell phone was invented in Israel by a Jewish engineer (and find another way to detonate planted explosives).

Meanwhile I ask, what medical contributions to the world have the Muslims made?"

The Global Islamic population is approximately 1,200,000,000; that is ONE BILLION TWO HUNDRED MILLION or 20% of the world's population.

They have received the following Nobel Prizes:

Literature:
1988—Najib Mahfooz

Peace:
1978—Mohamed Anwar El-Sadat

1990—Elias James Corey
1994—Yaser Arafat:
1999—Ahmed Zewai

Economics:
(zero)

Physics:
(zero)

Medicine:
1960—Peter Brian Medawar
1998—Ferid Mourad

TOTAL: 7 SEVEN

The Global Jewish population is approximately 14,000,000; that is FOURTEEN MILLION or about 0.02% of the world's population.

They have received the following Nobel Prizes:

Literature:
1910—Paul Heyse
1927—Henri Bergson
1958—Boris Pasternak
1966—Shmuel Yosef Agnon
1966—Nelly Sachs
1976—Saul Bellow
1978—Isaac Bashevis Singer
1981—Elias Canetti
1987—Joseph Brodsky
1991—Nadine Gordimer World

Peace:
1911—Alfred Fried
1911—Tobias Michael Carel Asser
1968—Rene Cassin
1973—Henry Kissinger
1978—Menachem Begin
1986—Elie Wiesel

1994—Shimon Peres
1994—Yitzhak Rabin

Physics:
1905—Adolph Von Baeyer
1906—Henri Moissan
1907—Albert Abraham Michelson
1908—Gabriel Lippmann
1910—Otto Wallach
1915—Richard Willstaetter
1918—Fritz Haber
1921—Albert Einstein
1922—Niels Bohr
1925—James Franck
1925—Gustav Hertz
1943—Gustav Stern
1943—George Charles de Hevesy
1944—Isidor Issac Rabi
1952—Felix Bloch
1954—Max Born
1958—Igor Tamm
1959—Emilio Segre
1960—Donald A. Glaser
1961—Robert Hofstadter
1961—Melvin Calvin
1962—Lev Davidovich Landau
1962—Max Ferdinand Perutz
1965—Richard Phillips Feynman
1965—Julian Schwinger
1969—Murray Gell-Mann
1971—Dennis Gabor
1972—William Howard Stein
1973—Brian David Josephson
1975—Benjamin Mottleson
1976—Burton Richter
1977—Ilya Prigogine
1978—Arno Allan Penzias
1978—Peter L Kapitza
1979—Stephen Weinberg
1979—Sheldon Glashow

1979—Herbert Charles Brown
1980—Paul Berg
1980—Walter Gilbert
1981—Roald Hoffmann
1982—Aaron Klug
1985—Albert A. Hauptman
1985—Jerome Karle
1986—Dudley R. Herschbach
1988—Robert Huber
1988—Leon Lederman
1988—Melvin Schwartz
1988—Jack Steinberger
1989—Sidney Altman
1990—Jerome Friedman
1992—Rudolph Marcus
1995—Martin Perl
2000—Alan J. Heeger

Economics:
1970—Paul Anthony Samuelson
1971—Simon Kuznets
1972—Kenneth Joseph Arrow
1975—Leonid Kantorovich
1976—Milton Friedman
1978—Herbert A. Simon
1980—Lawrence Robert Klein
1985—Franco Modigliani
1987—Robert M. Solow
1990—Harry Markowitz
1990—Merton Miller
1992—Gary Becker
1993—Robert Fogel

Medicine:
1908—Elie Metchnikoff
1908—Paul Erlich
1914—Robert Barany
1922—Otto Meyerhof
1930—Karl Landsteiner
1931—Otto Warburg
1936—Otto Loewi

1944—Joseph Erlanger
1944—Herbert Spencer Gasser
1945—Ernst Boris Chain
1946—Hermann Joseph Muller
1950—Tadeus Reichstein
1952—Selman Abraham Waksman
1953—Hans Krebs
1953—Fritz Albert Lipmann
1958—Joshua Lederberg
1959—Arthur Kornberg
1964—Konrad Bloch
1965—Francois Jacob
1965—Andre Lwoff
1967—George Wald
1968—Marshall W. Nirenberg
1969—Salvador Luria
1970—Julius Axelrod
1970—Sir Bernard Katz
1972—Gerald Maurice Edelman
1975—Howard Martin Temin
1976—Baruch S. Blumberg
1977—Roselyn Sussman Yalow
1978—Daniel Nathans
1980—Baruj Benacerraf
1984—Cesar Milstein
1985—Michael Stuart Brown
1985—Joseph L. Goldstein
1986—Stanley Cohen [& Rita Levi-Montalcini]
1988—Gertrude Elion
1989—Harold Varmus
1991—Erwin Neher
1991—Bert Sakmann
1993—Richard J. Roberts
1993—Phillip Sharp
1994—Alfred Gilman
1995—Edward B. Lewis
1996—Lu RoseIacovino

TOTAL: 129!

The Jews are NOT promoting brainwashing children in military training camps, teaching them how to blow themselves up and cause maximum deaths of Jews and other non-Muslims.

The Jews don't hijack planes, nor kill athletes at the Olympics, or blow themselves up in German restaurants.

There is NOT one single Jew who has destroyed a church.

There is NOT a single Jew who protests by killing people. The Jews don't traffic slaves, nor have leaders calling for Jihad and death to all the Infidels.

Perhaps the world's Muslims should consider investing more in standard education and less in blaming the Jews for all their problems.

Muslims must ask 'what can they do for humankind' before they demand that humankind respects them.

Regardless of your feelings about the crisis between Israel and the Palestinians and Arab neighbors, even if you believe there is more culpability on Israel's part, the following two sentences really say it all:

'If the Arabs put down their weapons today, there would be no more violence. If the Jews put down their weapons today, there would be no more Israel."

Benjamin Netanyahu: General Eisenhower warned us. It is a matter of history that when the Supreme Commander of the Allied Forces, General Dwight Eisenhower, found the victims of the death camps he ordered all possible photographs to be taken, and for the German people from surrounding villages to be ushered through the camps and even made to bury the dead.

He did this because he said in words to this effect: 'Get it all on record now—get the films—get the witnesses—because somewhere down the road of history some bastard will get up and say that this never happened'

Recently, the UK debated whether to remove The Holocaust from its school curriculum because it 'offends' the Muslim population which claims it never occurred.

It is not removed as yet. However, this is a frightening portent of the fear that is gripping the world and how easily each country is giving into it.

It is now more than 65 years after the Second World War in Europe ended.

Now, more than ever, with Iran, among others, claiming the Holocaust to be 'a myth,' it is imperative to make sure the world never forgets.

This e-mail is intended to reach 400 million people. Be a link in the memorial chain and help distribute this around the world.

How many years will it be before the attack on the World Trade Center 'NEVER HAPPENED' because it offends some Muslim in the United States?

Orville C. Green, BA, MDiv.
Clinical Fellow, AAMFT/OAMFT
Registered Marriage & Family Therapist
Individual & Relationship Counsellor
416.293.4760
www.aamft.org
www.ifl.on.ca

APPENDIX 4 TO CHAPTER 1

This Appendix is a verbatim reproduction of the Article published in the edition of STABROEK NEWS, October 27, 2012, Page 23. *(Given the thoughts expressed in this book about the concept of 'Stereotypes', it may be interesting to note that the Article, though about 'Sport', is printed cheek-by-jowl with the Table 'HOROSCOPES' by Holiday Mathis. Horoscopes have been cited in this book as a good example of 'Stereotyping'.)* The photograph of Roger Rajkumar that is part of the Article has not been reproduced here.

ARTICLE

Stabroek Sport

Canada-based Rajkumar back to defend title

Canada-based Guyanese golfer Roger Rajkumar has returned to defend his title in the fourth Annual Digicel two-day Golf Classic which tees off today at the Lusignan Golf Course.

Rajkumar arrived in Guyana Wednesday for this weekend's tournament but his main focus is on securing victory in the premier 2012 Banks DIH sponsored Guyana Open slated for November 4-5 at Lusignan.

Rajkumar was in striking range for championship honours at the prestigious Guyana Open last year but stumbled at the final hurdle in the tournament which was won by Trinidad—based Papo Haniff.

The experienced golfer said he has arrived early to work on his game ahead of the two major tours.

Apart from Rajkumar, four other overseas players Salim Rasheed, Andrew Claxton, Mo Saffie and Prem Ramnauth all from the United States will be in action this weekend.

The local players are also in tremendous form and will pose a serious challenge with the likes of three-time champion Avinesh Persaud, Alfred Mentore, Mohanlall Dinnanauth, Imram Khan, Mike Mangal, Kishna

Bacchus, William Walker, Colin Ming and Troy Cadogan being in contention.

Other leading contenders include Robert Hanoman, Patrick Prashad, Ayube Subhan, Fazil Deo, Chatterpaul Deo, David Harry, Munaff Arjune, Mike Guyadin, Lakeram Ramsundar and Sookram Deosarran.

The ladies competition is expected to be a two-player showdown between defending champion Christine Sukhram and Joaan Deo.

Jerome Khan, President of the Lusignan Golf Club said that the course is in immaculate condition so players can anticipate good scores.

Officials of Digicel including Managing Director Gregory Deane and Sponsorship manager Gavin Hope are expected to witness the two days of fierce competition.

Tee off is at 09:00 hours on both days.

End of Article.

CHAPTER 2

A National Assembly for Good Governance of Guyana

Chapter 1 has argued the case for treating the concept 'ethnicity based on race', especially in its application to the affairs of the Co-operative Republic of Guyana, as both otiose and pernicious. However, in the matter of the **Governance** of the Co-operative Republic of Guyana, some far more worrying dimensions arise for its National Assembly.

Governance of any Complex Adaptive System (CAS) requires the entity responsible for governance to identify and define the CAS's problems; and then to propose and implement solutions to those problems in a framework of systems thinking. The dimension of identification and definition of a problem is thus of fundamental importance in the activity of governing. The country often simply called 'Guyana' is a Complex Adaptive System.

I do not consider that in the matter of problem identification and solution proposal I can do better than refer to Chapter 4—The Problem and The Paradox—in the book entitled 'On Dialogue'. This book is based on the views expressed by David Bohm[31]; and I recommend that it be studied by anyone concerned with governance.

David Joseph Bohm (born 20 Dec 1917; died 27 Oct 1992), frequently referred to simply as David Bohm, was an American-born quantum physicist. For political reasons he acquired Brazilian and subsequently British citizenship. He has been considered one of the world's foremost theoretical physicists, neuropsychologists, and philosophers. In Chapter 4 of the book 'On Dialogue', Bohm is quoted as noting that *". . . . when one puts forth an idea in the form of a problem, there are certain largely tacit and implicit presumptions which must be satisfied if the activity is to make sense. Among these is of course the assumption that the questions raised are rational and free of contradiction. Sometimes, without our noticing it, we accept absurd problems with false or self-contradictory*

---

31 cf ON DIALOGUE, edited by Lee Nichol from the original material of the notes by David Bohm. It was first published in 1996 by Routledge, and later published in the Taylor & Francis e-Library, 2003.

presuppositions." This comment was made in the context of drawing a distinction between a **Problem** and a **Paradox**; and it was followed by the observation that *"It has to be emphasized, however, that as long as a paradox is treated as a problem, it can never be dissolved."*

Following this observation, Bohm remarked: *"Thus, for a long time, people sought to invent a machine capable of perpetual motion, but with the development of scientific understanding it became clear that this would be in contradiction with the basic laws of physics, and so the search for such a machine has ceased."*

I would like to think that after reading Chapter 1 of this book, it would be agreed by readers that the false or self-contradictory presuppositions associated with the concept 'ethnicity based on race' support the classification of the so-called 'race problem' in Guyana as a paradox rather than as a problem. Accordingly, as has been the case with the search for a perpetual motion machine, **all** institutions, and **especially** the National Assembly, should discontinue using physical, mental, and other resources in an attempt to solve the so-called 'race problem', regardless of the high political or intellectual rank of anyone who suggests that a solution to the alleged 'problem' is worthy of pursuit. Indeed, I recommend that the National Assembly should make, and cause to be enforced, legislation intended to ensure the discontinuance of the use of all categorizations related to the concept 'ethnicity based on race'.

Once a person becomes aware of the concept of 'race'/'ethnic group', and accepts their unique belongingness to any such group, they cannot avoid comparing themselves with other persons and other groups and the associated stereotypes that they have been taught exist. Awareness of 'race'/'ethnic group' is a necessary and sufficient condition for someone to have a racist view of the world. However, as Epictetus[32] had noted, though men are not responsible for the ideas that present themselves to their consciousness, they should be considered wholly responsible for the way in which they use those ideas.

Guyanese have been taught (by the formal and informal education system to which they have been exposed persistently as far back as colonial days) **to have a racist perspective on everything!** Accordingly,

---

32 Epictetus was a Greek political theorist and philosopher associated with the Stoics. His teachings reverted to the ideas of Socrates and Diogenes.

all members of the National Assembly need specific mental reconditioning and rehabilitation, and persistent stimulation, to resist racism in their thought processes, and consequently in their individual, collective, and collaborative efforts at decision-making.

This objective needs to be recognized and pursued if we are to be faithful to the spirit of Guyana's Constitution in the matter of governance, in accordance with the view expressed by Abraham Lincoln that *"The legitimate object of government is to do for a community of people whatever they need to have done, but cannot do at all, or cannot do so well, for themselves, in their separate and individual capacities."* L.F.S. Burnham, speaking immediately after the British Guiana elections of 1964,recognised this aspect of governance when in his Inaugural Speech he was moved to pronounce as follows: ***". . . . all the people of this country are equally important. . . . to us the Amerindians are important. . . . to us the Chinese are important . . . . to us the Portuguese are important . . . . to us the Europeans are important . . . . to us the mixed races are important . . . . to us the Africans are important . . . . to us the Indians are important".***

Burnham's pronouncement was **not** simply an oratorical exhortation! Burnham recognized the compulsions with which the led and the leaders of the emerging new nation had been endowed by the colonial experience and tutelage. He noted the futility of trying to derive a serious response to the question: ***'Who deh pan top?';*** or to the application of something analogous to the Hindu concept of caste. He recognized as inappropriate the uncivilized, un-Kama Sutra like, preference that 'deh-ing pan top' is perpetually the most desirable position for social intercourse. Accordingly, while agreeing that people are motivated by the natural instinct of individual and group self-preservation and self-interest, he subscribed to the view that the individual could not secure his own interests unless he participates as a contributor to the common welfare.

However, I do not think Burnham thought of or accepted what Bohm highlighted as the difference between a 'problem' and a 'paradox' with respect to the search for a solution. My conjecture is that he belonged to the group that thought the 'race problem' **was** a problem and ought to be solved! The members of the National Assembly currently appear to concur, and persist in treating this paradox as a problem.

In addition to the specific issues related to the so-called 'race problem', the National Assembly, if credibility is given to Bohm's distinction between a problem and a paradox, should develop a **general** capacity for determining whether any specific matter falls in the category 'paradox' as opposed to 'problem'. This capacity should continually be applied to ensuring that in the activity of defining problems related to governance and therefore requiring solutions, the National Assembly not waste resources, or indulge in exercises in futility. In this respect of problem identification, the National Assembly should also try to ensure that in defining problems they focus on root causes as opposed to dealing only with symptoms. The temptation to earn praise, with an eye on the next elections, by being seen to eradicate irritating symptoms, may be irresistible; but a focus on underlying systemic causes and their eradication should always be maintained. Adequate governance is not simply about palliatives. It demands identification and eradication of systemic causes, rather than repeated obliteration of uncomfortable symptoms those causes may generate.

In the second paragraph of this chapter, the assertion was made that the National Assembly, as the highest entity responsible for governance of Guyana, needs to propose solutions to the problems it identifies ***in a framework of systems thinking***. If this assertion is accepted as true, then by implication there should be acceptance also of the necessity for the National Assembly's work to be in accordance with the following:

(1) Decision-making should be based on 'dialogue' and **not** on 'debate';
(2) It should be recognized that pursuing the objective of a political party being politically 'pan top' is **not** the same as pursuing the objective of proposing what's best for governance of Guyana;
(3) Decision-making for good governance needs to depend on a systems thinking approach to: determining causation; utilisation of an unbiased, reliable, feedback mechanism dealing with the effects of adjustments made in the name of governance; and minimising the frequency of seizing opportunities in the National Assembly forum to indulge in heroification or demonization of individuals or political parties with an eye to winning future elections; and
(4) Ensuring that the National Assembly becomes a learning organization[33], at least in the sense of it not being presumed

33 I am using the term 'Learning Organization' in the same sense as Peter M. Senge uses it in his book 'The Fifth Discipline: The Art & Practice of The

that membership is evidence of wisdom[34], and that the Speaker adopts a facilitator's role in relation to the Assembly's learning as opposed to that of a referee imposed on warring factions each of which insists that it already 'knows'[35].

Each of the four types of conditionality just listed can benefit from much further discussion if the meaning and the expected results of their individual and joint application is to be fully understood.

With respect to the first conditionality, it is again useful to be guided by the ideas expressed by David Bohm as reported in 'On Dialogue'. My understanding is that in the pursuit of 'truth' or of what might best be done, it is useful to suspend acceptance or rejection of pre-determined ideas, not set out to prove them right or wrong, and in that state of suspension to discuss the ideas and their implications. Then, unlike what obtains in a debate, there is no pressure to win or lose and to utilize some kind of voting system[36]. In fact, in the context of a Party Whip kind of system in which individual members of the Assembly are directed how to vote, and may not vote otherwise regardless of what apprehensions they may have, in a two-party situation with 'no crossing of the floor' the Party with the majority in the National Assembly enjoys infallibility! The same specter of infallibility obtains when the National Assembly can be divided into Government and Opposition, with the Party in Government enjoying a majority of National Assembly membership. There is no opportunity for assessing, learning, and behaving in accordance with what has been learnt. Any attempt at dialogue is merely formal. In the debate, voting numbers rule. The façade of a decision-making process based on verbal presentations by Government and Opposition as opposing groups simply provides opportunities for public oratory and the temptation of pursuing the *frisson of schadenfreude.*

Learning Organization'.

34 As Epictetus allegedly said: 'It is impossible to learn that which one thinks one already knows.'

35 These factions, on the basis of Political Party Positions, usually have a predisposition to which application of the phrase coined by Fyodor Dostoyevsky in 'The Gambler' is appropriate—they exude '. . . . **an aggregate of conceit and gasconade'.**

36 This is a centuries old issue pronounced on, for instance, by Ramon Llull in his 'Art of Finding the Truth', written around 1283.

Also, the condition of colonial tutelage that by definition dominated the period prior to our attaining formal political independence ensured our predisposition to mimicry, apparently without serious consideration of relevance to the new objectives of governance. Thus, for instance, it appears that the appropriateness of the geometry of the chamber of the National Assembly to facilitate dialogue, as opposed to debate, was not considered as a major issue. A rectangular array of seating in confrontational rows was not discarded in favour of a non-rectangular (e.g. circular/elliptical?) array that might more facilitate the give and take of discussion to underpin dialogue and its reliance on mental exploration without the generation of heat and pomposity.

It is interesting to note that when a sports enthusiast visits any venue, the geometrical layout of the venue easily signals what sporting activity the venue is intended to facilitate. Thus, a cricket pitch does not signal that lawn tennis is about to be played. Similarly, a volleyball net does not signal the intention to play chess; nor do the lanes of an athletics track signal the intention to play any kind of football. In this vein, the geometry of the Chambers of the National Assembly signals the intention to encourage and facilitate the cut and thrust of contumelious debate, as opposed to sober exchanges of dialogue pursuing exploration of possible solutions to problems, while satisfying the requirements of the Constitution, with particular emphases on Article 13[37] and the Title 10 Interpretation of 'meaningful consultation' in section 232.

Indeed, there is an atmosphere of mimicry of the processes that the erstwhile most recent colonizers used to satisfy **their** objectives of governance. I am here reminded of the American Sioux word for 'white man'. The word is **'wasichu'** which means **'one who has everything good'**. We appear to have avidly embraced the colonial mechanisms of decision-making (mental and physical) for not dissimilar cultural imperialist 'wasichu' type reasons, even though we paid lip service to pursuit of the new objectives of an independent country.

---

37 Article 13 states: *The principal objective of the political system of the State is to establish an inclusionary democracy by providing increasing opportunities for the participation of citizens, and their organizations in the management and decision-making processes of the State, with particular emphasis on those areas of decision-making that directly affect their well-being.*

Readers may well consider my reference to cultural imperialism an unwarranted exaggeration. However, let me take the liberty of posing the following illustrative question: *What's so Guyanese about Guyana's National Anthem?* I would expect the answer to be sought by exploring the Guyaneseness of the lyrics and of the music[38].

The lyrics[39] do not recognize the reality of Guyana, by the time of independence in 1966, as being an ethnic melting pot not capable of being accurately described as 'One land of six peoples'. Cultural syncretism had already manifested itself, and such a description could be considered as inappropriate as an already cooked pot of cook-up rice being described as a dish of 'x' ingredients. It can be argued that the lyrics of the National Anthem should not be supportive of 'Race/Ethnicity' being a Guyanese obsession á la Willie Lynch's strategy of divide and rule.[40] Also, perhaps with the support of poetic licence and overweening aspiration, each of the four stanzas ends with a reference to Guyana being a land of the free—a comforting delusion in this world of the pursuit of international political influence?

However, one may note that though national anthems are usually in the most common language of the country, there are some notable exceptions:

- **India**'s anthem, *Jana Gana Mana* is in a highly Sanskritized version of Bengali;
- **Switzerland**, with four official languages *(French, German, Italian, and Romansh)* has different lyrics for each of the languages;
- **Canada**, with English and French as its official languages, has different lyrics for both languages, and sometimes mixes stanzas from its French and English versions; and
- **New Zealand**'s national anthem has the first verse in *Maori*, and the second in *English* sung to the same tune without the words being a direct translation of each other!

38 The Anthem was selected a month before Independence in 1966.

39 The stanzas of Guyana's National Anthem are stated in the Appendix 1 to this Chapter.

40 'Divide and Rule' was a tried and tested strategy used by the Spanish to defeat the Aztecs in Mexico; and the English used it in Scotland and Ireland, playing tribes against one another to extend British rule.

There therefore was precedent for Guyana's National Anthem to have achieved the uniqueness of a stanza in some Amerindian language (e.g. Arawak or Warrau or Wapishiana or any of the other six)[41] and the rest in English.

In the matter of the music, the composer should be expected to have been at liberty to prescribe all elements of music, including tempo, agogics, modalities, and the instruments to be used. In Guyana's case, that liberty appears to have been used to simply accept the immanent universality of world empire in Western Music. This choice appears to have been made without the benefit of research into the music of the coastal Amerindians of Guyana—the Arawak, Carib and Warrau—of the type done much later by ***David Blair Stiffler*** to underpin the recordings and annotations in FOLKWAYS RECORDS Album No.FE4239.

However, the composer ***(Robert Cyril Gladstone Potter)*** did not appear to have indulged in, or to have been required to pursue the curiosities of the kind Stiffler had, in pursuit of including in our National Anthem any kind of folk dimension, including an indigenous one. Thus, for instance, there appears to have been no flirting with the use of the pentatonic scale *(do-re-mi-sol-la-do)* often found in folk music, or with the use of musical instruments tuned to utilize that scale. It cannot have been that a musical approach of the kind that would have inculcated the Guyanese folk dimension was too radical a departure from tradition.

For instance, as far back as in 1893, Antonin Dvorak's *New World* Symphony, the Symphony No.9 in E Minor, glorified the American and the Czech folk spirit through the use of syncopations, pentatonic scales and other scales often found in folk music, and received popular acclaim in America. Dvorak had in 1892 gone to New York and had spent almost three years as director of the National Conservatory of Music, during which he had encouraged American composers **to write nationalistic music**.

The national anthems of **Japan** (Kimi ga Yo), of **Kenya** (Ee Mungu Nguvu Yetu), of **Bhutan** (Druk tsendhen), and of **Nepal** (Sayaun Thunga Phool Ka) use pentatonic scales. Further, in the musical matter of modality, the

41 cf the Stabroek News Article '*Arawak language revival project launched in Capoey*' of Thursday, September 19, 2013, and the follow up Editorial of Sunday, September 22, 2013.

national anthem of South Africa, and that of Italy do not start and end in the same key.

My own conjecture is that the Guyanese political and cultural powers that were in 1966 did not deliberate seriously on how the lyrics and the music of a national anthem for Guyana might be endowed with uniqueness. I suspect that neither Archibald Leonard Luker, who authored the lyrics, nor R.C.G. Potter, who composed the music, was given any specific guidance on the matter of pursuing uniqueness. My conjecture is that the political and cultural powers preferred the conservative 'respectability' of indulging in the mimicry of colonialism as to how a National Anthem should sound; even while they paid lip service to the cultural importance of the indigenous people. In this respect they were not different from their English-speaking Caribbean counterparts and contemporaries[42]! There appears to have been an exercise in cultural xenophilia (focused on so-called 'classical' music?), about how a National Anthem should sound.

Quite coincidentally, this conjecture was reaffirmed in my mind when I read the letter to the Stabroek News of Thursday, August 29, 2013 by Hamilton Green, then Georgetown's mayor, a previous Prime Minister of Guyana, and one of the leading political figures at the time of Guyana's Independence. My perceived reaffirmation is based on the presumption that in relation to music, the effect of the opening of one's pores and the filling of one's heart with joy depend on the degree and direction of acculturation which one has accepted. The letter, captioned ***'Our young people need to explore the exciting world of music'***, is reproduced as Appendix 2 to this Chapter.

The point made about the probable lack of uniqueness of Guyana's National Anthem may well be categorized, and consequently dismissed, as a trivial observation. However, that uniqueness may be important in relation to:

- the need for a new country to be geared to give concerted effort to agreeing a unique national vision;
- mustering the creative conceptual effort to pursue that vision; and

42 I understand that in the case of Trinidad & Tobago, on becoming independent in 1962, they simply adopted the national anthem *(Forged from the Love of Liberty)* that was originally composed as the national anthem for the West Indies Federation which lasted from 1958 to 1962.

- generating what Hamilton Green's letter described as a 'pore opening' emotional response to participating in the national development effort (a kind of national battle cry)[43].

In the matter of agreeing a unique national vision, I am particularly attracted to Arnold Schoenberg's approach to musical composition in which, having taken the revolutionary step of abandoning the traditional tonal system, he pursued use of the Twelve-Tone System. I am assured that in twelve-tone composition, all pitches are derived from a special ordering of the twelve chromatic tones (each ordering being referred to as a tone row); and that the choice of rows is practically limitless, since there are 479,001,600 possible arrangements of the twelve chromatic tones. I consider the freedom of choice afforded by this kind of limitlessness to be analogous to what is required mentally to develop, and proselytize, a new unique national vision, particularly if that vision is not slavishly going to mimic the vision of some other nation.

Another important deficiency in the process of decision-making by the National Assembly appears to be its minimal utilization of systems thinking. This cannot be the appropriate place to attempt to deal with the detail of how systems thinking might be applied to Guyana's National Assembly; and with how the Assembly might become a Learning Organization. A much better approach is for me to encourage persons interested in the matter to acquire and study Peter M. Senge's book 'The Fifth Discipline: The Art & Practice of the Learning Organization.'[44] I recommend particularly PART III The Core Disciplines: Building the Learning Organization which begins with the following paragraph about a necessary condition: ***"Organizations learn only through individuals who learn. Individual learning does not guarantee organizational learning. But without it no organizational learning occurs."*** It also highlights the importance of being in a continual learning mode, and of people sharing a common vision.

The following concluding chapter of this book highlights some issues and ideas that could be worth pondering in pursuit of the objective of having Guyana's National Assembly evolve into a Learning Organization.

---

43 That is the basis on which the Tradewinds song *'Not a Blade of Grass'* has been described as Guyana's 'second' National Anthem as a response to Venezuela's territorial claim.

44 The original edition of this book was published in 1990. A new, revised edition was published some 15 years later. It is available as an ebook.

APPENDIX 1

Lyrics of Guyana's National Anthem

Dear land of Guyana,
of rivers and plains
Made rich by the sunshine,
and lush by the rains,
Set gem-like and fair
between mountains and sea—
Your children salute you,
dear land of the free.

Green land of Guyana,
our heroes of yore
Both bondsmen and free,
laid their bones on your shore;
This soil so they hallowed,
and from them are we,
All sons of one mother,
Guyana the free.

Great land of Guyana,
diverse though our strains,
We are born of their sacrifice,
heirs of their pains,
And ours is the glory
their eyes did not see—
One land of six peoples,
united and free.

Dear land of Guyana,
to you will we give
Our homage, our service,
each day that we live;
God guard you, great Mother,
and make us to be
More worthy our heritage—
land of the free.

The National Pledge

I pledge myself to honour always the flag of Guyana, and to be loyal to my country, to be obedient to the laws of Guyana, to love my fellow citizens, and to dedicate my energies towards the happiness and prosperity of Guyana.

APPENDIX 2

What follows is the verbatim text of the letter by Hamilton Green, published under the title: 'Our young people need to explore the exciting world of music' on page 6 of the STABROEK NEWS, Thursday, August 29, 2013.

"Dear Editor,

This reflection is not a criticism of anyone, but rather a petition on behalf of our children and our beloved country, even as we agonize over the 'lost art of expressing ourselves" (see *Stabroek News*, August 27,p13). The world knows how powerful a force music is; any civilized society needs to promote an appreciation of music (not amplified noise) let us hear the difference.

Last Sunday evening I attended a concert titled 'Bach to Baroque,' featuring the Trinidad and Tobago Youth Philharmonic Orchestra made up of just under two hundred youths from five years to twenty-three years of age coming from different schools. They were brought together with their instruments, and had spent fifteen days of intense practice (9am to 4pm).

It was tough but rewarding; they were divided into Junior, Intermediate and Advanced categories, but my pores opened and my heart was filled with joy as I listened to these youngsters perform with gusto and excellence: violins, cellos, violas, flutes, clarinets, double basses, oboes, bassoons, trumpets, tubas, timpani, percussion all in harmony and unison produced sweet, dulcet melodies, with no PA system.

My music teacher a long time ago reminded us of an old saying: "Music when healthy is the teacher of perfect order, also when depraved is the teacher of perfect disorder."

In Guyana we need perfect order beyond this; there is no good reason why this sort of activity should not be at least to honour our departed musical stalwarts: 'Uncle' Percy and 'Aunt' Ivy Loncke, Enid Peters, Shirley Garraway, the Dolphin sisters, the McDavids, PM De Weever, Major Henwood, Director of the then Militia Band, Barney Small, Peter Koulen, Eleanor Kerry, Jane Hunter, Mrs Jordan, Lucille Dewar, Maurice Watson, Harry Whittaker, Lynette Katchey, George Noel, WRA 'Billy' Pilgrim, Valerie Rodway, MA Cossou, Jodina, RCG Potter, Sonny Ault, W Hawley Bryant, Horace Taitt and a host of others still with us such as, Hilton Hemerding, Hugh Sam, Ray Luck, Eddy Grant, Frank Daniels and others abroad.

Holding the fort at home and giving us hope, we have Dr Wendy Rudder, Professor Joycelyn Loncke and family, Marilyn and David Dewar, Michael Basdeo, Asst Commissioner Bovell and other music teachers.

Money? Guyana with its gold, diamonds, timber and marine resources is not short of money, but the powers that be must make massive investment in our youth in this important area of our culture music.

What we need is a vision, some set of persons or person to put aside personality, profits and policies to give our young people an opportunity to explore the exciting world of music, to be creative and to learn to love by playing good music together. How else can we build a solid and safe future? Let them fiddle with fiddles not drugs and danger.

Why should we permit our natural resources to be exploited by aliens and those who could not care beyond their money bags?

My dream is to experience the same joy in Guyana as I did on Sunday at the Queen's Hall, Port of Spain. Can we do it? Yes we can! Our Government can take the lead; ensure that music is taught in every school—a pianoforte in each school as a beginning. I hope the two provided at President's College in 1987 are still in place.

Yours faithfully,
Hamilton Green, JP

CHAPTER 3

Issues and Suggestions re Guyana's National Assembly

If I were required to compile a list of issues relevant to the matter of the National Assembly of Guyana being transformed into a Learning Organisation, then at, or close to, the top of that list would be the issue of the Assembly's formal use of feedback mechanisms. Here, I am referring to the Assembly's deliberate construction and use of some mechanisms that would apprise it promptly and accurately of the results of the implementation of decisions made by the Assembly, with a particular focus on the deviation of actual from intended results. I would also be referring to the Assembly's willingness to revisit those decisions, and to adjust them as it deemed necessary, on the basis of the variance between the observed and the originally intended results.

The ideas expressed above, and indeed many of those that will be expressed in and underpin the rest of this Chapter, derive from my assumption that the National Assembly is responsible for governance of the Complex Adaptive System (CAS) called Guyana. The analogue of a person being responsible for driving a motor car (in that sense governance of the car) is then intuitively relied upon.

The driver of the car is assumed to have clarified the vision of where the car and its occupants wish to go, and by when they wish to reach their destination. The driver is assumed to have accepted the responsibility of getting them there safely, regardless of how the driver was chosen. In discharging this responsibility, the driver relies on a number of feedback mechanisms.

These feedback mechanisms include the instrument panel (the dashboard) of the car. The dashboard provides the driver with information such as what distance he has so far travelled, how much fuel he has left, the vital signs of engine wellness (e.g. engine temperature; engine oil level), and a clock. On the basis of this kind of dashboard information, which the driver can access on a continual basis, and other relevant information, he governs the car in pursuing the objective of delivering his passengers to a defined location by a target time.

In relation to the National Assembly, it having defined the Guyana vision in accordance with the Constitutional requirements and procedures regarding consultation etc., the Assembly should specifically define the feedback mechanisms it proposes to use. My suggestion is that these mechanisms should include mandatory inputs by the institutions whose business is informing the general public about what is going on in Guyana. Accordingly, these institutions would include **all** newspapers, and they would be required as a mandatory aspect of performance under the terms of their individual licences to jointly apprise the Assembly formally, with an agreed reporting periodicity, about matters that they and the Assembly have agreed need to be monitored in the pursuit of good governance.

Once the feedback reports have been received by the Assembly, the Assembly shall be empowered to require from specific institutions, especially the University of Guyana, adequately researched technical advice. This technical advice should focus on the adjustments that should be made by the Assembly to any aspects of its governance decisions that appear to correlate with the variances between actual results and the results originally intended by the Assembly.

In order to have members of the National Assembly apprised promptly of all that is taking place, and to facilitate the smooth working of the feedback system, appropriate Information Technology devices (e.g. Internet linked tablets) should be supplied and pressed into service; and communication procedures and systems to facilitate decision-making should be established, together with a system of penalties for not using them. The analogous situation with respect to driving the car is that the driver is not at liberty to ignore dashboard information, especially warnings, and unexpected occurrences!

The point has been made that a Learning Organisation has to treat learning as a continuous exercise, with no position of having learnt all that is required ever being reached. In support of such a stance by the National Assembly, a number of organizations that supply feedback information to the Assembly would have to adopt continuous learning stances similar to that of the National Assembly.

Among the organizations that I would expect to fall into that category would be the Elections Commission. Given the role that we appear to not be able to avoid giving to 'voting' in our decision-making processes, there needs to be continual monitoring of the complexities associated with voting as a basis for decision-making. There is no shortage of academic literature that focuses on aspects of this matter; nor of actual country experience (e.g. The Brazilian experience). In these circumstances it should appear not unreasonable for the Elections Commission to be required to establish a Research Unit to provide feedback to the Assembly, both proactively and reactively as the Assembly deems necessary.

Such feedback should pertain to not only National or Regional Elections and their satisfaction of criteria blessed constitutionally as desirable (e.g. representativeness on the basis of age, or gender, or geography)[45]; but more widely to the issues of the efficacy of decision-making by voting. Nevertheless there may be much merit in requiring emphasis to be given to the application of computer based technology to the conduct of both National and Regional Elections.

I suspect that the application of computer technology to the information communication requirements of the National Assembly in the mode of a learning organization can generate: cost savings; time efficiencies in the distribution of decision-making information; and avoidance of governance pitfalls referable to the preferences and interests of a plutocracy. Dialogue will also be encouraged and facilitated. Most importantly, conditions shall have been created for revising the memes with which Guyanese, particularly members of the National Assembly, have been imbued by decades of mis-education.

It is appropriate to end this chapter, and thereby close this book with the following important caveat. In each of the areas dealt with in this concluding chapter, there should be serious research done into the dimensions of organizational appropriateness, efficiency, and cost effectiveness prior to any attempted implementation. Indeed, given the risks associated with resistance to system change, Ovid's advice may be apposite. Stated in its original Latin, that advice is: ***Aut non tentaris, aut perfice***. When translated it means: '**Either do not attempt, or else succeed**.'

---

45 A good example may be the use by the Elections Commission of a measure like the Gallagher Index to measure the disproportionality of an electoral outcome to guide the Assembly in its decisions about the sizes and compositions of Parliamentary Committees.

ABOUT THE AUTHOR

William, Haslyn, Parris (born 2 March, 1941), facilitated by two scholarships he won in 1959—one to UCWI, Jamaica, and the other the Guiana Scholarship—obtained degrees in Mathematics (BSc Special, UCWI, Mona—1962); Economics (BSc. Hons—1966, LSE); and Economics specializing in Statistics (MSc—1967, LSE).

His career has encompassed the positions of Mathematics Teacher at Queen's College (1962-1963), Senior Economist at the Central Bank of Guyana (1967-1969), Chief Economist of the Central Bank of Guyana (1969-1971), Chief Executive Officer, Guybau and subsequently Guymine (1971-1981), Chairman of Guyconstruct (1976-1980), Chairman of the Bauxite Industry Development Company, BIDCO (1982-1983), Deputy Chairman of the State Planning Commission (1977-1983), Chairman of the State Planning Commission (1983-1991), and Deputy Prime Minister responsible for Planning and Development (1984-1991).

During the 24 year period (1967-1991), Mr Parris played key roles in the negotiations that led to the nationalizations of the bauxite companies Demba (1971), and Reynolds in Berbice (1975); which gave rise to Guybau, Bermine, and subsequently their merger Guymine. He lived through the systemic consequences of those nationalizations in the position of being responsible for the running of the bauxite industry as its Chief Executive Officer.

He was subsequently involved in designing divestment strategies, and in divestment negotiations, initiating those for the bauxite and sugar industries, and completing those for the national Telephone Company, and Demerara Woods Limited. He also undertook the negotiations which led to the 50/50 joint venture between Reynolds and the Government of Guyana—Aroaima Mining Company Ltd.

Early in the 1970's he became a member of the Central Executive of the then ruling People's National Congress, and continued to be a member of that Party until 1991. the more than a quarter of a century of intimate exposure to academic, public sector and private sector business activities (including being on Boards of several companies), and politics, has provided the author with interesting insights into the economic development process, both nationally and internationally (all gained at ringside or in the ring so to speak).

On 1 May, 1991, Mr. Parris demitted office as Deputy Prime Minister, having achieved 50 years and several academic and other awards such as the 'Daily Chronicle 1971 Man of the Year', the most prestigious being the national award, Cacique Crown of Honour (C.C.H.) in 1980. He opted for a private life in the private sector, and currently is a member of the Board of Omai Gold Mines Ltd.

Mr. Parris has been involved in a number of matters concerning the Constitution of Guyana. These matters have included: the negotiations leading to the Herdmanston Accord (17 Jan 1998); the Constitution Reform Commission of which he was Secretary (1999); the Oversight Committee on Constitutional Reform (1999 / 2000) as Coordinator; and as one of the Commissioners of the Guyana Elections Commission (2001)—a post he demitted on 31 July, 2006.

He has published several books, including: Two Volumes of Ribald Tales of Guyana; Bunaro (a set of essays on economic development relevant to Guyana); The Constitution of Guyana: What will it look like?; an Annotated Handbook of the 17 July 1999 Report of The Constitution Reform Commission of Guyana;1992-2003 Heretical Musings about Guyana; and Parris Electoral Conjectures and Governance in Guyana.

END